BASKETBALL
SUPERSTARS
2019

JON RICHARDS

CARLTON
KiDS

THIS IS A CARLTON BOOK
Text, design, and illustration © Carlton Books Limited 2019

This edition published in 2019 by Carlton Books Limited, an imprint of
the Carlton Publishing Group, 20 Mortimer Street, London W1T 3JW

Written by Jon Richards
Designed by Tall Tree Ltd

Special thanks to Eric Hoffman and Bret Hoffman

ISBN: 978-1-78312-408-4

Printed in China

CONTENTS

NBA 2018 SEASON

With the drafts complete and the ink dry on the contracts it's time to get down to the serious stuff as the **2018–19 NBA SEASON** gets underway. Over the next **NINE MONTHS,** some of the biggest sports stars on the planet will battle it out for glory and the **NBA CHAMPIONSHIP.**

WHO GOES WHERE?

While the 2018 NBA draft is sure to uncover some new gems who will shine on the court, there are still plenty of veterans and seasoned campaigners who are sure to influence the outcome. How will LeBron James perform now that he's left the Cleveland Cavaliers and moved on to the L.A. Lakers? Can Kyle Lowry drive the Raptors to the finals this year, and will Victor Oladipo (*left*) push for MVP honors in his second year at the Pacers? It's going to be a thrilling ride! So hold onto your hats as we show you some of the biggest stars in the NBA!

DRAFT AND BEYOND!

The 2018 NBA draft threw up few surprises as the Phoenix Suns and the Sacramento Kings claimed the first two picks, selecting Deandre Ayton and Marvin Bagley respectively. In other developments, the Nuggets have unveiled a new logo for the season, hoping that will change their fortunes. Meanwhile, the NBA looks to spread its international influence with the announcement that the Mavericks and the 76ers will play two preseason games in China.

WARRIORS OR CAVS?

The 2017–18 season saw the Golden State Warriors defeat the Cleveland Cavaliers in the NBA finals to clinch their second title in a row. Can Stephen Curry, Kevin Durant, and the rest of the team repeat the achievement and make it a hat trick of consecutive titles? Or will the Cavaliers have other ideas? One thing you can be certain of—the other teams will have something to say about the matter. Maybe the Celtics and the Spurs could go one better this year and reach the finals themselves. Or perhaps the challenge will come from elsewhere? Maybe the Mavericks and the Suns can dig themselves out of the league's basement with some clever drafting and dealing.

CHRIS PAUL

Now in his **14TH SEASON IN THE NBA,** you might think that Chris Paul would be slowing down. But that's the last thing on his mind! With devastating changes of pace, **DEFT HANDLING,** and great court vision, he is still one of the **BEST PERIMETER DEFENDERS IN THE GAME,** and more than a match for any new kids on the block!

PAUL
3

HOUSTON ROCKETS | POINT GUARD

D.O.B: MAY 6, 1985 | **HEIGHT:** 6'0" | **WEIGHT:** 175 LBS
DEBUT: vs. SACRAMENTO KINGS, NOVEMBER 1, 2005 (93–67 WIN)
GAMES: 892 | **POINTS PER GAME:** 18.7 | **ASSISTS PER GAME:** 9.8

COLLEGE DEMON

Paul thrived at high school in North Carolina, where he became a McDonald's All-American, and even managed to score 61 points in a single game. He moved on to Wake Forest University, helping to guide the college's Demon Deacons team to their first-ever number one ranking. He was named Atlantic Coast Conference (ACC) Rookie of the Year in 2004 and broke the record for assists, drawing the attention of several NBA teams.

TRADE TIME

Desperate to sign a player of Paul's quality, the Houston Rockets traded seven players, a future first round pick, and a load of cash to get their man from the Clippers in 2017. However, injury limited Paul to only 58 games that season. Even so, he helped to guide the Rockets to the finals, where, with Paul forced to sit out the last two games, they were eliminated by the Golden State Warriors. In his star-studded career, Paul has been a nine-time NBA All-Star, made the All-NBA Team eight times, and was even voted NBA All-Star Game MVP in 2013.

HITTING THE BIG TIME

The New Orleans Hornets swooped on Paul in the 2005 NBA draft, making him the fourth pick in the first round. And he didn't disappoint! In his first season, he averaged 36 minutes of game time for the 78 games he played, all as a starter, notching 16.1 points per game and leading all rookies in points, steals, assists, and double-doubles—no wonder he was voted NBA Rookie of the Year! In 2011, he moved west to join the Los Angeles Clippers and his performances didn't drop off. In partnership with teammates Blake Griffin and DeAndre Jordan, the Clippers developed a fast-paced offense centered on alley-oop dunks that earned them the nickname "Lob City."

Paul faces off against Gary Harris of the Denver Nuggets during a game in February 2018.

⟫⟫⟫⟫ FAST FACT ⟫⟫⟫⟫

As part of a powerful Team USA, Chris won two gold medals at the Summer Olympic Games in Beijing in 2008 and London in 2012.

DAMIAN LILLARD

Lillard is well-known for his **AMAZING HANDLING,** great movement, and a burning desire to win. And he's taken that desire to the Portland Trail Blazers, where **"BIG GAME DAME,"** who may only be in his eighth season with the NBA, is on track to become one of the **ALL-TIME GREAT POINT GUARDS** in the game.

LILLARD
0

PORTLAND TRAIL BLAZERS | POINT GUARD

D.O.B: JULY 15, 1990 | **HEIGHT:** 6'3" | **WEIGHT:** 195 LBS
DEBUT: vs. LOS ANGELES LAKERS, OCTOBER 31, 2012 (116–106 WIN)
GAMES: 469 | **POINTS PER GAME:** 23.1 | **ASSISTS PER GAME:** 6.2

SCHOOL AND COLLEGE

As one of the stars of the Oakland High School team, Lillard averaged 22.4 points and 5.2 assists per game in his senior year. He moved to Weber State University in Ogden, Utah, leading the team to an impressive 21–10 record. At Weber State, he became the Wildcats' second-highest scorer of all time and the fifth-highest scorer in the history of the Big Sky Conference with 1,934 points. Deciding to forego his senior year, he became the sixth overall pick in the 2012 NBA draft, joining the Portland Trail Blazers. An amazing first NBA season saw him claim the NBA Rookie of the Year crown.

POINT TO PROVE

In October 2017, he passed the 9,000 point mark, becoming the fastest Blazer to do so, in just 402 career games. And he didn't slow down. During a February 2018 game against the Sacramento Kings, he scored a season-high 50 points—in just 29 minutes! His scoring success helped to guide Portland to the playoffs, where they were eliminated in the first round by the Pelicans. Even so, Lillard's performances earned him selection to the All-NBA First Team, becoming only the third player in Blazers history to win first team honors, after Bill Walton (1977–78) and Clyde Drexler (1991–92).

Lillard leaps to shoot over the outstretched arms of Houston Rockets guard Eric Gordon during the third quarter at the Moda Center.

KEEPING ON

His second season saw Lillard score 1,695 points, helping the Blazers reach the Western Conference semifinals. It also led to his first All-Star selection on the All-NBA Third Team. His performances went from strength to strength and, before the 2015–16 season, the Blazers offered him an eye-watering five-year contract worth $120 million. Lillard enjoyed a record-breaking 2016–17 season. During a January 2017 game, he reached 8,000 NBA points and 2,000 assists, becoming only the third player after LeBron James and Michael Jordan to do so in their first five seasons.

>>>>> **FAST FACT** >>>>>

Lillard wears the number 0 on his jersey. It also represents the letter O for his journey from Oakland to Ogden and then on to Oregon.

STEPHEN CURRY

With his trademark jump shot, rapid release, and **STUNNING ACCURACY,** Steph Curry is the best shooter currently operating in the NBA. He has led the NBA **FOUR TIMES** in free throw percentage and is the Warriors' all-time free-throw leader— little wonder they offered him a record-breaking **$201-MILLION DEAL** in July 2017.

CURRY
30

GOLDEN STATE WARRIORS | POINT GUARD

D.O.B: MARCH 14, 1988 | **HEIGHT:** 6'3" | **WEIGHT:** 190 LBS
DEBUT: vs. HOUSTON ROCKETS, OCTOBER 28, 2009 (108–107 LOSS)
GAMES: 625 | **POINTS PER GAME:** 23.1 | **ASSISTS PER GAME:** 6.8

FATHER'S FOOTSTEPS

Stephen Curry is the son of Dell Curry, a lethal shooting guard who played for the Jazz, Cavaliers, Hornets, Bucks, and the Raptors. Steph entered the unheralded Davidson College in 2006. In 2008–09, he led all college juniors nationwide in scoring 28.6 points per game to help take the Davidson Wildcats to the NCAA regional finals. He became (and remains) Davidson's all-time points scorer with 2,635. His final season at college saw him average 5.6 assists and 2.5 steals per game, as well as becoming the NCAA scoring leader. He opted out of his final college year and entered the 2009 NBA draft.

MAKING A SPLASH

Curry is one half of a backcourt pairing with Klay Thompson. Nicknamed the "Splash Brothers," the pair have smashed the record for most three-pointers in a season for three seasons in a row. In 2016–17, they became the first duo to both record over 200 three-pointers a season for five straight seasons. Steph also set a new NBA record with 13 three-pointers in a single game—a 116–106 win over the New Orleans Pelicans in November 2016.

Curry drives past Lonzo Ball of the Lakers as he helps the Warriors on to a 123–127 victory.

>>>>>> FAST FACT >>>>>>

Curry's jersey was the best-selling NBA jersey in three seasons from 2015–18. His endorsements have made him one of the world's highest-paid celebrities.

GOLDEN-STATE GLORY

In 2014–15, Steph scored 1,900 points as the Warriors won their first NBA Championship since 1974–75. He was made NBA MVP, a feat he repeated the next season when he became the first MVP to win by a unanimous vote—fair reward for a stellar season. Although the Warriors were overturned by the Cleveland Cavaliers in the 2015–16 final, they stormed back the following year, making Curry a two-time champion. Things got better during the 2017–18 season, and Steph topped it off by scoring 37 points in game four of the finals as the Warriors brushed aside the Cavaliers for Curry's third title.

RUSSELL WESTBROOK

A left-hander who shoots right-handed, Russell is known to **ATTACK THE RIM,** but will also hold back to fire off medium-range jump shots, or look to create a **SCORING CHANCE** for his teammates. His range of skills have seen him selected as an NBA **ALL-STAR SEVEN TIMES** (2011, 2012, 2013, 2015, 2016, 2017, 2018) and made **ALL-STAR MVP** twice (2015, 2016).

OKLAHOMA CITY THUNDER | POINT GUARD

D.O.B: NOVEMBER 12, 1988 | **HEIGHT:** 6'3" | **WEIGHT:** 200 LBS
DEBUT: vs. MILWAUKEE BUCKS, OCTOBER 29, 2008 (98–87 LOSS)
GAMES: 748 | **POINTS PER GAME:** 23.0 | **ASSISTS PER GAME:** 8.2

FROM SCHOOL TO COLLEGE

When he started playing for his high school team, Westbrook was only 5'8" tall and weighed just 140 pounds. His small size saw him overlooked for much of his school career, until a growth spurt one summer took him to 6'3". He caught the attention of UCLA, where he managed to secure a place on the highly rated Bruins team. During his two years with the Bruins, he was used as a starter less than half the time, and only started one game in his junior year. Even so, he entered the 2008 NBA draft and was fourth pick for the Seattle SuperSonics. Six days later, the team relocated to Oklahoma City as the Thunder.

RISING THUNDER

Westbrook soon earned a reputation for his athleticism and energy at both ends of the court. During his time with the Thunder, he developed an intimidating partnership with Kevin Durant which helped to power the Thunder to the Western Conference finals four times in six years, and to the NBA finals in 2011–12. He has the fifth highest number of assists of any active player. In 2014–15, he led the league in points per game, notching 1,886 points at an average of 28.1 per game, and went even better in the 2016–17 season by averaging 31.6 points per game.

STUNNING SEASON

During the 2016–17 season, Westbrook recorded five 50-point or more games and broke Oscar Robertson's 1961–62 season record for the most triple-doubles, collecting 42. If that wasn't enough, he also averaged 10.4 assists and 10.7 rebounds per game. No wonder he was named the NBA season MVP! After that kind of performance, the Thunder didn't hesitate to offer him a five-year $205 million contract extension in 2017. And he didn't wait to start paying them back on the investment, leading the NBA in assists with 10.3 per game and guiding the Thunder to the playoffs at the end of the 2017–18 season.

Westbrook powers past Mario Chalmers of the Grizzlies to slam home another two points.

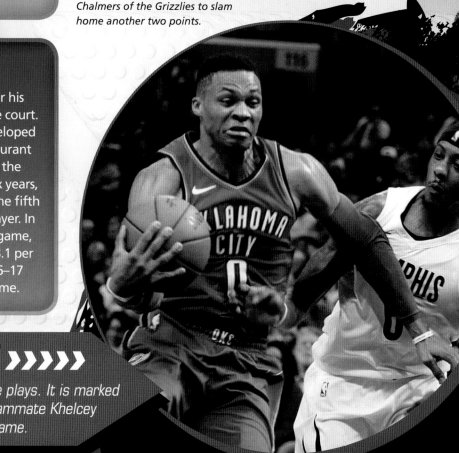

>>>>> FAST FACT >>>>>

Westbrook wears a wristband when he plays. It is marked "KB3" in honor of his friend and college teammate Khelcey Barrs, who died after collapsing during a game.

BIGGEST DUNKS

Get ready to rise above the rest of the crowd! Scoring plays don't get any bigger than a **SLAM DUNK**—and these are the biggest and best dunks by the biggest and best players from the **LAST 12 MONTHS!** Prepare to be amazed as these players **FLY, LEAP, SOAR,** and generally **DEFY GRAVITY** on their way to the hoop.

GIANNIS ANTETOKOUNMPO

MATCH: MILWAUKEE BUCKS vs. DETROIT PISTONS

DATE: NOVEMBER 3, 2017

With the Pistons defense arranged tightly in front of the hoop, Giannis receives a pass from Malcolm Brogdon on his unfavored left hand. With only one thing on his mind, Giannis decides he doesn't want to waste time going around the defense, so he chooses to go over them and launches himself at the hoop—two points!

JAYLEN BROWN

MATCH: BOSTON CELTICS vs. NEW YORK KNICKS
DATE: JANUARY 31, 2018

Defending deep under their own net, Al Horford intercepts a wayward pass and launches a fastbreak counterattack down the court. One, two, three, four bounces take him clear down the other end of the court, where a short pass puts Jaylen Brown into the clear to launch himself at the Knicks hoop and slam home the two-pointer.

LARRY NANCE JR.

MATCH: L.A. LAKERS vs. GOLDEN STATE WARRIORS
DATE: DECEMBER 18, 2017

You'll believe a man can fly when you see this dunk. Nance Jr. just seems to hang in the air as he soars over no less a player than Kevin Durant to slam the ball home clean through the net!

LAURI MARKKANEN

MATCH: CHICAGO BULLS vs. NEW YORK KNICKS
DATE: JANUARY 10, 2018

Twenty-year-old rookies just shouldn't be able to do this! Driving in from the right-hand side of the court, Finnish sensation Markkanen brushes aside one Knicks defender before leaping over Enes Kanter to score the dunk and swing on the ring. Oh, and he also managed a career-best 33 points that night—this boy will go far!

JAMES HARDEN

Harden is one of the NBA's **TOP SCORERS** and many rate him as the **BEST SHOOTING GUARD** in the game. So it's no surprise that he's earned five **ALL-NBA TEAM** honors and he finished 2018 by claiming that season's **MVP** award for the very first time.

HOUSTON ROCKETS | SHOOTING GUARD

D.O.B: AUGUST 26, 1989 | **HEIGHT:** 6'5" | **WEIGHT:** 220 LBS
DEBUT: vs. SACRAMENTO KINGS, OCTOBER 28, 2009 (89–102 WIN)
GAMES: 687 | **POINTS PER GAME:** 23.0 | **ASSISTS PER GAME:** 6.1

SCHOOL STAR

During his time at Artesia High School in Lakewood, California, Harden led his team to two state titles. In his final year he finished with 18.8 points, 7.9 rebounds, and 3.9 assists per game as Artesia finished the year 33–2. Moving on to Arizona State University, Harden proved just as effective and his efforts in his junior year saw him named first team All-Pac-10 and to the conference freshman team. He ended his sophomore year with averages of 20.1 points, 5.6 rebounds, and 4.2 assists and was named Pacific-10 Conference's Player of the Year, before declaring for the 2009 NBA draft.

THUNDER AND ROCKETS

Harden was picked third overall by the Oklahoma City Thunder and went to work right away. He achieved the most consecutive three-point makes by a rookie since Michael Dickerson in 1999 and was named to the NBA All-Rookie Second Team. The following year, he recorded more than 10 points in 54 matches and kept pushing things the next season, averaging 16.8 points, 4.1 rebounds, and 3.7 assists per game on his way to winning the NBA Sixth Man of the Year Award as the best-performing player to come off the bench. However, contract disputes at the end of the season saw Harden traded to the Rockets in October 2012.

Harden soars to tip the ball over two Timberwolves defenders during an NBA playoffs match in February 2018.

›››› FAST FACT ››››

Harden *started growing his beard in 2009 because he was too lazy to shave. It's so famous now that it appears on t-shirts and has even been mentioned in songs!*

STARTING ROLE

Moving into the Rockets' starting lineup, Harden got off to a flying start and ended the 2012–13 season as only the fourth player to score 600 free throws and more than 150 3-pointers in a single season. Season after season, Harden's performances improved. In 2014–15, he helped the Rockets to their first division title since 1994. He made even more history in the 2015–16 season when he joined LeBron James, Michael Jordan, and Oscar Robertson as the only players in NBA history to average more than 29 points, 7 assists, and 6 rebounds in a season.

DONOVAN MITCHELL

He may have spent just **ONE SEASON** in the NBA, but Donovan Mitchell knows how to **MAKE AN IMPACT**, raising the bar and setting records **ACROSS THE LEAGUE.** This explosive athlete excels across the board in **PASSING,** shooting, rebounding, and **DEFENDING,** proving that he really is the **FUTURE OF THE NBA.**

UTAH JAZZ | SHOOTING GUARD

D.O.B: SEPTEMBER 7, 1996 | **HEIGHT:** 6'3" | **WEIGHT:** 215 LBS
DEBUT: vs. DENVER NUGGETS, OCTOBER 18, 2017 (106–96 WIN)
GAMES: 79 | **POINTS PER GAME:** 20.5 | **ASSISTS PER GAME:** 3.7

ROUTE TO THE DRAFT

In high school, Mitchell excelled at both basketball and baseball. But a broken wrist forced him to drop baseball and focus on basketball. As a result of this and his performances on the court, he drew the attention of several colleges, opting to play for the University of Louisville. During his second year, he averaged 2.7 assists, 4.9 rebounds, and 15.6 points per game, earning a place on the First Team All-Atlantic Coast Conference. He opted out of college after that season, choosing to make himself available for the 2017 NBA draft.

INSTANT IMPACT

Mitchell made an instant hit in the Jazz lineup. He recorded 10 points and four assists in his very first game against the Denver Nuggets. Then on December 1, 2017, he scored a career-best 41 points against the Pelicans, setting the Jazz scoring record for a rookie and becoming the first rookie to score more than 40 points since Blake Griffin in 2011. And things just kept getting better. On January 15, 2018, he broke Karl Malone's record for most 20+ games in a rookie season when he recorded his 19th of the year.

BETTER AND BETTER

In February 2018, he won a slot in the NBA Slam Dunk Contest after Aaron Gordon had to pull out. He then went on to become the first rookie to win the competition since Zach LaVine in 2015. He went on to set a new record for the most 3s in a rookie season, with 186, before leading the Jazz into the playoffs. During the first round against the Oklahoma City Thunder, he set a record for points scored by a shooting guard in the first two postseason games, breaking Michael Jordan's record by scoring 55 points. In May 2018, he finished the season by being named to the NBA All-Rookie First Team.

Mitchell slams home another two points against the Cleveland Cavaliers in December 2017.

▶▶▶▶▶ FAST FACT ▶▶▶▶▶

Mitchell wears the number 45 on his jersey out of respect for NBA legend Michael Jordan, who wore the number for his baseball career and at the start of his NBA comeback.

FROM WAY DOWNTOWN

NOTHING BUT NET— that's all you'll hear when these guys are **ON THE ATTACK.** And don't think they need to be right **UNDER THE HOOP** to score. Drop your guard for one second and it's **"SWISH"**— three points!

J.J. REDICK

TEAM: PHILADELPHIA 76ERS
POSITION: SHOOTING GUARD

Having made a name for himself at Duke University (where he still holds the all-time points scoring record), Redick has had a stellar career first with the Magic, and then with stints at the Bucks and Clippers, before ending up with the 76ers. During one game in November 2017, he recorded an astonishing 8-of-12 from three-point range in a 121–110 win over the Pacers.

VICTOR OLADIPO

TEAM: INDIANA PACERS
POSITION: SHOOTING GUARD

With a reputation for hard work and detailed preparation before a game, Oladipo combines a powerful athletic approach with amazing leaping ability to score dunk after dunk for the Pacers. And he's not bad from distance either, posting a three-point conversion average of .353 over his NBA career.

C.J. McCOLLUM

TEAM: PORTLAND TRAIL BLAZERS

POSITION: SHOOTING GUARD

McCollum had to wait his turn before he could shine in the NBA. Despite being made Patriot League Men's Basketball Player of the Year in both 2010 and 2012 and being selected by the Trail Blazers as the 10th overall pick of the 2013 NBA draft, he had to spend two seasons as a reserve before he became a full-time starter.

BRADLEY BEAL

TEAM: WASHINGTON WIZARDS
POSITION: SHOOTING GUARD

With a three-point field goal percentage of .393, Beal is a master of the court from long-range. In fact, he's so good that, in November 2017, he became the youngest player in NBA history to reach 700 made three-pointers. And the following month, he scored five three-pointers on his way to scoring a career-best 51 points against Portland. Small wonder he was picked as an NBA All-Star in 2018!

LEBRON JAMES

LeBron James is the NBA's **BIGGEST STAR.** He is athletic, explosive, and, at times, impossible to defend against. In his 15 seasons in the NBA, he has become a **THREE-TIME NBA CHAMPION,** been selected as an **NBA ALL-STAR 14 TIMES,** and been made NBA MVP for four seasons. And if that's not enough, he's also won two **OLYMPIC GOLD MEDALS.**

JAMES 23

L.A. LAKERS | SMALL FORWARD

D.O.B: DECEMBER 30, 1984 | **HEIGHT:** 6'8" | **WEIGHT:** 250 LBS
DEBUT: vs. SACRAMENTO KINGS, OCTOBER 29, 2003 (106–92 LOSS)
GAMES: 1,143 | **POINTS PER GAME:** 27.2 | **ASSISTS PER GAME:** 7.2

FROM PREP TO PRO

Growing up in Akron, Ohio, LeBron enjoyed all sports at school and excelled in two especially: football and basketball. As a wide receiver, he was so good for his high school football team, that he was named to the All-State First Team. But basketball took over, and he led his high school team to three Ohio state championships in four seasons, being named "Mr. Basketball" in the state for three seasons in a row. James decided to skip out college altogether, and was chosen by the Cavs as the very first pick in the 2003 draft.

SCORING GREAT

No matter where he plays, James scores big and breaks records. He became the youngest player to reach 5,000 NBA points, 10,000 NBA points, 15,000 NBA points, 20,000 NBA points, 25,000 NBA points, and even 30,000 NBA points. In 2014, James became a free agent and returned to the Cleveland Cavaliers. Since his return, they've reached the NBA finals four times in a row (2015–2018), winning the championship in 2016. During the 2017–18 season he became only the second player in NBA history, after Michael Jordan, to score 10 or more points for 800 games in a row.

THE DECISION

LeBron smashed records as soon as he entered the NBA, becoming the youngest rookie named as starter aged just 18 years, 303 days. With the Cavaliers, he reached the NBA finals in 2007, and won the 2009 and 2010 NBA season MVP awards. In 2010, however, he became a free agent and could sign for any team. He decided to announce he was joining the Miami Heat in a TV special called *The Decision*, a move that angered many fans. James enjoyed success with the Heat, winning back-to-back championships in 2011–12 and 2012–13, and being named finals MVP on both occasions.

James dunks to score a basket against Team Stephen during the second half of the 2018 NBA All-Star Game.

>>>>> FAST FACT >>>>>

In July 2018, he stunned the NBA world by announcing a four-year $154 million deal that saw him move west as a free agent to join the L.A. Lakers.

KEVIN DURANT

Kevin Durant has won pretty much all there is on the court. He's a two-time Olympic **GOLD MEDALIST** and a FIBA World Championship gold medalist and **MVP.** For the NBA, he's a **TWO-TIME CHAMPION** and Finals MVP, and a **NINE-TIME** NBA All-Star (2010–18). And with **27.1 POINTS-PER-GAME** average through his career, he has one of the highest NBA scoring rates of all time.

DURANT
35

GOLDEN STATE WARRIORS | SMALL FORWARD

D.O.B: SEPTEMBER 29, 1988 | **HEIGHT:** 6'9" | **WEIGHT:** 240 LBS
DEBUT: vs. DENVER NUGGETS, OCTOBER 31, 2007 (120–103 LOSS)
GAMES: 771 | **POINTS PER GAME:** 27.1 | **ASSISTS PER GAME:** 3.9

INTO THE BIG LEAGUE

Growing up in Maryland, Durant had something of a head start over other high school players—literally! By the age of 13–14, he was already 6'0" tall and he went on to play for Amateur Athletic Union (AAU) teams in his area. After high school, he played just one year of college basketball with the Texas Longhorns, winning the Naismith College Player of the Year, an award previously won by Michael Jordan. In honor of his college achievements, the Longhorns retired his #35 shirt. In a rush to play in the biggest league of all, he entered the 2007 draft and was picked by the Seattle SuperSonics—who became the Oklahoma City Thunder a season later.

CHAMPION AND MVP

But there was one thing missing in Durant's prize cabinet—an NBA Championship. So in 2016, he moved to join Steph Curry, Klay Thompson, and a host of other top-rate players at the Golden State Warriors. It paid dividends right away. In the 2016–17 playoffs, Durant was the top scorer in every game, leading the Warriors to the NBA Championship against the Cavaliers. The very next year, the Warriors repeated the feat, with Durant winning a second NBA Finals MVP award.

>>>>> FAST FACT >>>>>

Kevin has contributed articles and photographs to new media sports platform The Players' Tribune. He's also tried acting, appearing in the 2012 movie Thunderstruck.

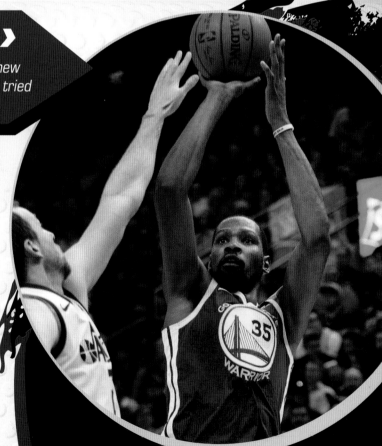

Utah Jazz forward Joe Ingles tries to stop a shot from Durant during the NBA playoffs in April 2018.

LETHAL MARKSMAN

Durant is one of the league's great shooters, able to fire off effortless soaring jump shots, power to the basket on drives, and pop up with rebounds and fadeaway jumpers in the post position. He has led the NBA in points in four separate seasons, scoring 2,593 points in 2013–14, the most since Kobe Bryant in 2005–06, and was also named the NBA MVP in 2014. He reached the championship final in the 2011–12 season, only to lose to LeBron James's Miami Heat.

JAYSON TATUM

He may be new to the NBA, but being a rookie hasn't held Jayson Tatum back. His performances in the **REGULAR SEASON** saw him play a key part in the Celtics' **STARTING LINEUP.** And he saved his best for the season **PLAYOFFS,** earning himself a selection to the **NBA ALL-ROOKIE FIRST TEAM.**

TATUM
0

BOSTON CELTICS | SMALL FORWARD

D.O.B: MARCH 3, 1998 | **HEIGHT:** 6'8" | **WEIGHT:** 205 LBS
DEBUT: vs. CLEVELAND CAVALIERS, OCTOBER 17, 2017 (99–102 WIN)
GAMES: 80 | **POINTS PER GAME:** 13.9 | **ASSISTS PER GAME:** 1.6

EARLY PROSPECT

While in high school, Tatum excelled for both the Chaminade College Preparatory School Red Devils and the AAU St. Louis Eagles on the Nike Elite Youth Basketball Circuit. During his senior year, he averaged 29.6 points and 9.1 rebounds per game, and recorded six 40-point games. His performances earned him selection to the 2016 McDonald's All-American Game and he was named the 2016 Gatorade National Player of the Year. By the end of his high-school career, he was rated a five-star recruit and ESPN rated him their number three overall player. He committed himself to Duke University.

FROM COLLEGE TO NBA

During his freshman year, Tatum averaged 16.8 points and 7.3 rebounds per game, helping the Blue Devils clinch the ACC Tournament Championship with a 75–69 victory over the Notre Dame Fighting Irish. After they were defeated by the University of South Carolina in the second round of the NCAA Tournament, Tatum chose to opt out of the rest of his college career and made himself available for the 2017 NBA draft where the Celtics chose him as the number 3 pick overall.

Tatum soars above Jazz forward Jonas Jerebko in March 2018, helping the Celtics on to a 94–97 victory.

OUT OF THE BLOCKS

In his very first game for the Celtics, Tatum posted a double-double with 14 points and 10 rebounds against the Cavaliers and went on to be named the Eastern Conference Rookie of the Month for December. He started 80 games during his rookie season, helping to guide the Celtics to a 55–27 record and into the playoffs. In his first playoff game, Tatum posted another double-double and went on to score 20 or more points in three of the seven first-round games as the Celtics beat the Bucks. In the second round against the 76ers, Tatum became the first Celtics rookie to post 25 or more points since Larry Bird in 1980.

>>>>> FAST FACT >>>>>

At the end of the 2017–18 playoffs, Tatum joined Kareem Abdul-Jabbar as the only rookies to score 20 or more points in 10 games of their first playoff run.

GREATEST OF ALL TIME

Just how do **TODAY'S SUPERSTARS** compare to some of the greatest that have ever stepped on a court? Compare two **MODERN GREATS** with a couple of **TITANS OF YESTERDAY** and see if you can decide who comes out **ON TOP.** Or perhaps you've got some other superstars in mind?

KOBE BRYANT

D.O.B: AUGUST, 23, 1978
POSITION: SHOOTING GUARD
TEAMS: L.A. LAKERS

A player so good that Reuters described him as "the best player of his generation," Kobe Bryant has achieved everything. He's a five-time NBA champion, 18-time NBA All-Star, winner of the NBA Slam Dunk Contest, and he scored 33,643 points at a rate of 25.0 points per game. And to cap it all, he's even won an Oscar for his short movie *Dear Basketball*.

VS

STEPHEN CURRY

D.O.B: MARCH 14, 1988 | **POSITION:** POINT GUARD | **TEAMS:** GOLDEN STATE WARRIORS

No team is safe when the ball is in Curry's hands, whether it's under the rim or close to halfway. He's the Warriors' all-time free-throw leader, with a conversion rate of more than 90 percent. In fact he's so dangerous, that many teams double-team him just to try to keep him quiet, leaving time and space for Curry's teammates to grab the glory!

LEBRON JAMES

D.O.B: DECEMBER 30, 1984 | **POSITION:** SMALL FORWARD | **TEAMS:** CAVALIERS (TWICE), HEAT, LAKERS

Starting as an 18-year-old rookie, James made an immediate impact, leading the Cavaliers in scoring in his first season. Since then, he's won everything there is to win, and is one of only five players to win four or more MVP awards. This guy really is one of the greats—and he's still playing!

VS

MICHAEL JORDAN

D.O.B: FEBRUARY 17, 1963
POSITION: SHOOTING GUARD
TEAMS: CHICAGO BULLS (TWICE), WASHINGTON WIZARDS

What can you say about this man? He had a jump that defied gravity and earned him the nickname "Air Jordan," which is still used to brand sneakers. He was also in such demand that he came out of retirement not once, but twice. He won five MVP Awards and held ten scoring titles, and still holds the records for regular and post season scoring averages —could he be the greatest ever?

ANTHONY DAVIS

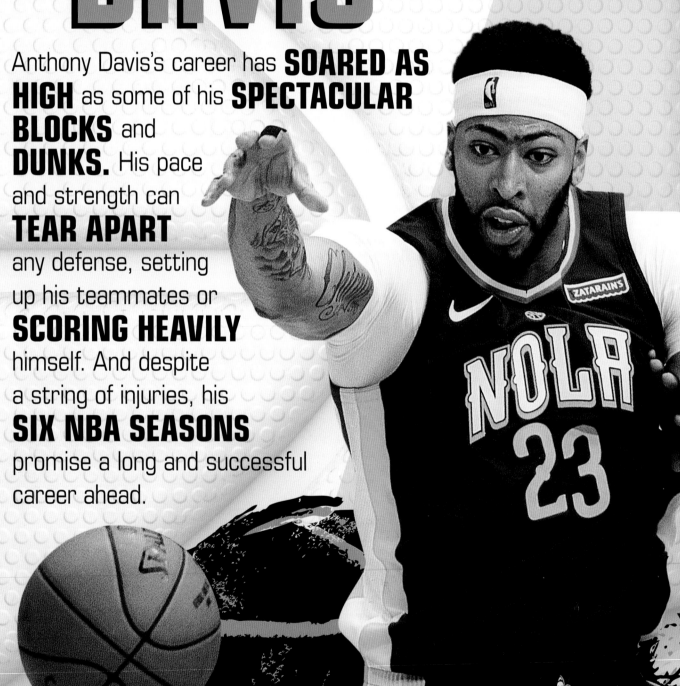

Anthony Davis's career has **SOARED AS HIGH** as some of his **SPECTACULAR BLOCKS** and **DUNKS.** His pace and strength can **TEAR APART** any defense, setting up his teammates or **SCORING HEAVILY** himself. And despite a string of injuries, his **SIX NBA SEASONS** promise a long and successful career ahead.

DAVIS 23

NEW ORLEANS PELICANS | POWER FORWARD

D.O.B: MARCH 11, 1993 | **HEIGHT:** 6'10" | **WEIGHT:** 253 LBS
DEBUT: vs. SAN ANTONIO SPURS, OCTOBER 31, 2012 (99–95 LOSS)
GAMES: 410 | **POINTS PER GAME:** 23.4 | **ASSISTS PER GAME:** 1.9

POINTS EXPLOSION

Anthony started his competitive career at Perspectives Charter School, and underwent a seven-inch growth spurt in his teens, before joining the University of Kentucky. Davis starred as the Kentucky Wildcats won their eighth NCAA championship and, with it, a glut of college basketball player-of-the-year awards. It was no surprise that he entered the June 2012 NBA draft as the number one pick.

PLAYOFF SPECIALIST

Davis may have only reached the playoffs twice with the Pelicans, in 2015 and 2018, but he always seems to save his best for this part of the season. In the four games of the 2015 playoff, he averaged 31.5 points per game and across the nine games of the 2018 playoffs he scored 30.1 points per game, before the Pelicans were defeated over five games in the second round by the Golden State Warriors.

FAST STARTER

Six weeks after joining the New Orleans Pelicans (then the Hornets), Anthony found himself as part of the 2012 Olympic gold medal–winning US team, after replacing Blake Griffin on the roster. In his debut NBA season, he started 60 out of 64 games played, scoring 867 points and making 112 blocks, to be named to the NBA All-Rookie First Team. He also finished second in the voting, behind Damian Lillard, for the NBA Rookie of the Year award. The following season, Davis led the league in blocks made per game with 2.8 (a feat he improved on in 2014–15 with 2.9) and upped his points per game from 13.5 in his rookie season to 20.8. Season after season, he has increased his scoring rate, peaking in 2017–18 with a rate of 28.1 points per game and leading the NBA in blocks per game for this season with an average of 2.6 per game.

Davis in action on the way to scoring 37 points against the Dallas Mavericks in March 2018.

>>>>> FAST FACT >>>>>

In 2017, Davis was named NBA All-Star Game Most Valuable Player after scoring 52 points to set a new All-Star Game record.

DRAYMOND GREEN

Some people think that Draymond Green is a little **SHORT** to be a power forward. But that hasn't stopped him from driving the Warriors to **THREE NBA TITLES.** On the way he's become a three-time **NBA ALL-STAR,** been selected twice for All-NBA, **LED THE LEAGUE** in steals (2017), and was voted 2017 NBA Defensive Player of the Year.

GREEN
23

GOLDEN STATE WARRIORS | POWER FORWARD

D.O.B: MARCH 4, 1990 | **HEIGHT:** 6'7" | **WEIGHT:** 230 LBS
DEBUT: vs. PHOENIX SUNS, OCTOBER 31, 2012 (87–85 WIN)
GAMES: 467 | **POINTS PER GAME** 9.3 | **ASSISTS PER GAME** 4.6

POWERING FORWARD

During his senior year playing for Saginaw High School in Saginaw, Michigan, Green recorded an average of 20 points, 13 rebounds, and two blocked shots per game, leading the team to an impressive 27–1 record. Committing to Michigan State University, he spent most of his first two years coming off the bench for the Spartans. By the time he was in his senior year, he was captaining the team, leading them to victory in the Big Ten Tournament. For his efforts that year, he was named the Big Ten Player of the Year by the coaches and journalists.

GOLDEN WARRIOR

At the 2012 NBA draft, the Warriors made Green the number 35 pick overall. However, he had to be patient and got very little court time during the first part of his rookie season. Things improved a little as the Warriors pushed into the playoffs, where they were knocked out in the second round by the Spurs. Throughout the 2013–14 season, Green played a total of 82 games, with 12 as a starter, and earned praised for his tough defense. The following season proved a breakout year for Green, as he was promoted to the starting lineup in what became a championship winning team.

In 2017, Green became the NBA Steals Leader for making the most number of steals in a single season.

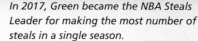

》》》》 FAST FACT 》》》》

Green finished his college career with Michigan State as one of only three players in Spartans' history to score more than 1,000 points and register over 1,000 rebounds.

STRENGTH TO STRENGTH

The 2015–16 season may have been something of a disappointment for Warriors fans as they lost in the finals to the Cavaliers, but Green took his chance to build on his previous year. In March 2016, during a win over the Utah Jazz, he became the first player in NBA history to record 1,000 points, 500 assists, 500 rebounds, 100 steals, and 100 blocks in a season. For the next two seasons, Green proved a central player as the Warriors marched to two consecutive titles, earning himself a third consecutive NBA All-Star selection.

GIANNIS ANTETOKOUNMPO

"The Greek Freak" is nicknamed for his **7'3" WINGSPAN** (the distance between his outstretched arms) and incredible skills for a big man. These skills mean that, while he plays mainly as a **FORWARD** for the Bucks, he can also turn his hand at **GUARD.** In 2016–17, he became the **FIRST PLAYER** in NBA history to finish a regular season in the top 20 in total points, rebounds, assists, blocks, and steals.

ANTETOKOUNMPO
34

MILWAUKEE BUCKS | POWER FORWARD

D.O.B: DECEMBER 6, 1994 | **HEIGHT:** 6'11" | **WEIGHT:** 222 LBS
DEBUT: vs. NEW YORK KNICKS, OCTOBER 30, 2013 (90–83 LOSS)
GAMES: 393 | **POINTS PER GAME:** 17.2 | **ASSISTS PER GAME:** 3.8

FROM GREECE TO MILWAUKEE

The son of Nigerian parents, Charles and Veronica, who moved to Greece in 1991, Giannis was born in Athens and grew up playing basketball with his four brothers. Moving up through the youth ranks of Greek club Filathlitikos B.C., he became part of the senior team in 2012, joining his older brother, Thanasis, and would later be joined by his younger sibling, Kostas. Some clubs in Europe coveted the young player, but he made himself available for the 2013 NBA draft where he was selected as a first-round pick by the Milwaukee Bucks.

SUPER START

Antetokounmpo became the youngest player to make his NBA debut in the 2010s. He was so young that he was still growing when he joined the NBA, and now stands 2½ inches taller than when he was drafted. In his first season, he scored double figures in 23 games and finished the season with 61 blocks, more than any other rookie that year. In 2014, he played for Greece at the FIBA Basketball World Cup and, a year later, took part in the NBA Slam Dunk Competition. The 2014–15 season saw him help the Bucks to the playoffs where they lost in the first round to the Chicago Bulls.

Giannis celebrates another successful dunk, this time against the Sacramento Kings in November 2017.

LEARNING HIS CRAFT

Giannis enjoyed a stellar 2016–17 season, ending the regular season first for his club in all five major categories with an average 22.9 points, 8.8 rebounds, 5.4 assists, 1.9 blocks, and 1.6 steals per game. He became only the fifth player in NBA history to lead his team in all five categories, the last being LeBron James in 2008–09, helping the Bucks back to the playoffs once again. And he's gone on to improve his game, pushing his points average for the 2017–18 season to a career high of 26.9 points per game.

>>>>> FAST FACT >>>>>

Giannis's handspan—measured from the tip of the thumb to the tip of the little finger—is 12 inches; that's 2¾ inches bigger than LeBron James's hands.

IT'S A TEAM GAME

The people on these pages may not be the **STARS OF THEIR TEAMS** and they may have had a harder time **REACHING THE NBA.** But they do show that there's more than one way of **HITTING THE BIG TIME,** whether it's **SHOOTING HOOPS** on the court or **SUPPORTING THEIR TEAM** off it.

LUC RICHARD MBAH A MOUTE

TEAM: L.A. CLIPPERS
POSITION: SMALL FORWARD

Mbah a Moute really is basketball royalty—he's an actual prince from the village of Bia Messe in Cameroon and the son of the elected village chief! His 10 seasons in the NBA have seen him on the move, taking him to Milwaukee, Sacramento, Minnesota, Philadelphia, Los Angeles, Houston, and now back to L.A.

KHRIS MIDDLETON

TEAM: MILWAUKEE BUCKS

POSITION: SHOOTING GUARD

After a quiet rookie season with the Pistons, where he only played in 27 games, Middleton was traded to the Bucks where he has gone on to become a key part of the team. In fact, during the 2017–18 season, he started every single one of the Bucks' 82 games, posting 5.2 rebounds, 4.0 assists, and 20.1 points per game, as well as a career-high 43 points against the Charlotte Hornets in November 2017.

AL HORFORD

TEAM: BOSTON CELTICS

POSITION: CENTER

Horford enjoyed nine fruitful seasons with the Atlanta Hawks, after being selected as the third overall pick of the 2008 NBA draft. With his contract having run out, he became a free agent in 2016 and chose to move to Boston, where he signed a colossal $113 million four-year contract to become part of the Celtics team.

KYLE KORVER

TEAM: CLEVELAND CAVALIERS

POSITION: SHOOTING GUARD

Now in his 16th season in the NBA, Korver is a true veteran having had stints with the 76ers, Jazz, Bulls, Hawks, and now the Cavaliers. During his career, he has led the NBA in three-point and free throw percentages, and still holds the three-point field goal conversion record, posting .536.

KARL-ANTHONY TOWNS

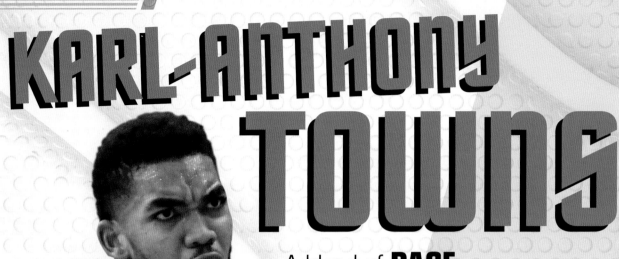

A blend of **PACE, STRENGTH, AND SKILL,** Karl-Anthony Towns is a powerful defensive force, capable of making multiple blocks. He has an average of **11.7 REBOUNDS** per game in his first three NBA seasons. But there's much more to his game, as shown by his high numbers of steals and blocks, and an NBA career average of **21.6 POINTS PER GAME.**

TOWNS
32

MINNESOTA TIMBERWOLVES | CENTER

D.O.B: NOVEMBER 15, 1995 | **HEIGHT:** 7'0" | **WEIGHT:** 248 LBS
DEBUT: vs. LOS ANGELES LAKERS, OCTOBER 28, 2015 (112–111 WIN)
GAMES: 246 | **POINTS PER GAME:** 21.6 | **ASSISTS PER GAME:** 2.4

HIGH-SCHOOL STAR

Towns was an early starter and was even picked to represent the Dominican Republic (where his mother is from) at the 2011 FIBA Americas Championship when he was only 16 years old. As a high-school star, Towns led his team to three state titles in 2012, 2013, and 2014. It was also in 2014 that Karl-Anthony won the Gatorade National Basketball Player of the Year—the ultimate award for a high-school player, and awarded in the past to LeBron James and Kobe Bryant. On graduating from high school, he opted to play for the Kentucky Wildcats. After just one year at the college, he impressed NBA scouts enough that the Minnesota Timberwolves snapped him up in the 2015 NBA draft.

HISTORY-MAKER

Karl-Anthony stepped up his game in 2016–17, adding 6.8 points to his points-per-game average, as well as over 150 more rebounds. By the end of the season, he had made NBA history as the only player to score more than 2,000 points (finishing with 2,061 in total), 1,000 rebounds (1,007), and 100 three-pointers (101) in the same season. Anthony kept his standards high for the 2017–18 season, matching his average rebounds per game from the last year (12.3) and guiding the Timberwolves into the playoffs for the first time since 2004.

≫≫≫ FAST FACT ≫≫≫

Karl-Anthony studied kinesiology (body movement) at college and he plans to become a doctor when his basketball career is over.

Towns outpowers his way past New Orleans center Demarcus Cousins in January 2018.

FITTING IN

The 7-foot-tall center with a 7'4" wingspan became the first draft pick of the 2015–16 NBA and slotted straight into the starting lineup. One of just 18 NBA players to start all 82 games of the regular season, Karl-Anthony led all rookies that season in points scored and rebounds. After winning all six Rookie of the Month awards in the Western Conference, Towns was unanimously voted NBA Rookie of the Year, and also scooped the NBA All-Star Weekend Skills Challenge.

JOEL EMBIID

With a career that's been **PLAGUED BY INJURY,** Joel Embiid has had to be patient to make his mark in the NBA. But when he's **FULLY FIT,** there are few opponents who can handle this **NATURALLY GIFTED** and strong athlete with good hands and a soft touch who came to the sport at a relatively **LATE AGE.**

EMBIID
21

PHILADELPHIA 76ERS | CENTER

D.O.B: MARCH 16, 1994 | **HEIGHT:** 7'0" | **WEIGHT:** 250 LBS
DEBUT: vs OKLAHOMA CITY THUNDER, OCTOBER 26, 2016 (103–97 LOSS)
GAMES: 94 | **POINTS PER GAME:** 22.0 | **ASSISTS PER GAME:** 2.8

AFRICAN DISCOVERY

Growing up in Yaoundé, Cameroon, Embiid initially wanted to make a career as a professional volleyball player in Europe. However, when he was 15, a chance discovery at a basketball camp by fellow Cameroonian and NBA recruit Luc Mbah a Moute pushed Embiid to change his mind. With Mbah a Moute encouraging and mentoring the young player, he moved to the USA and, ultimately, high school in Gainesville, Florida. In his senior year, he posted an average of 13.0 points, 9.7 rebounds, and 1.9 blocks, leading his team to a season record of 33–4. He committed to the University of Kansas in 2013.

RISING STAR

During his one and only college season, Embiid recorded an average of 11.2 points and 8.1 rebounds per game over his 28 games. He was named as a finalist for the Naismith College Player of the Year, earned Big 12 Defensive Player of the Year honors, and was named to the All-Big 12 second team. However, he suffered a setback in March 2014 following a stress fracture to his back that ruled him out of that year's Big 12 tournament and the NCAA tournament—it was the start of a long struggle against injury. Even so, Embiid declared for the 2014 NBA draft as the 76ers made him the third overall pick.

Embiid keeps possession of the ball, helping secure a 120–97 win against the Brooklyn Nets in March 2018.

LONG WAIT

Before he'd even stepped onto an NBA court, Embiid underwent surgery to repair a broken bone in his foot. But complications and slow healing ruled him out for not one, but two entire years, and he had to wait for the 2016–17 season to make his first NBA start. In March 2017, a knee injury ruled him out for the rest of the season, but that didn't stop him from earning selection to the NBA All-Rookie First Team. The following year, Embiid managed to start all 63 games he played in, posting 22.9 points and 11.0 rebounds per game on his way to selection for his first All-Star game.

>>>>> FAST FACT >>>>>

When Embiid was picked in the 2014 NBA draft, he became only the third player from Cameroon selected to play in the league.

RUDY GOBERT

This French international's incredible wingspan makes him a **FORMIDABLE** defensive opponent. His 2016–17 displays saw him selected for the **2017 ALL-NBA SECOND TEAM.** His performances during the 2017–18 season earned him the **LOCKSMITH PRIZE** from the National Basketball Players Association, making him their defensive player of the year.

GOBERT
27

UTAH JAZZ | CENTER

D.O.B: JUNE 26, 1992 | **HEIGHT:** 7'1" | **WEIGHT:** 245 LBS
DEBUT: vs. OKLAHOMA THUNDER, OCTOBER 30, 2013 (101–98 LOSS)
GAMES: 325 | **POINTS PER GAME:** 10.0 | **ASSISTS PER GAME:** 1.2

FRENCH CONNECTION

Rudy was born in the northern French town of Saint-Quentin and brought up by his mother, Corinne. His father, Rudy Bourgarel, played for the French national basketball team in the 1980s. Gobert moved away from home at age 15 to play pro basketball with French club Cholet. In 2010, he starred at the FIBA Europe Under-18 Championship where he was France's top scorer and rebounder. Graduating to the French national team, Rudy won bronze medals at both the 2014 FIBA Basketball World Cup and EuroBasket 2015.

TRADING PLACES

After three years with Cholet, Rudy declared himself available for the 2013 NBA draft, where he was picked in the first round by the Denver Nuggets, who later traded him to the Jazz. Though the French rookie played a part in 45 NBA games in his first season, he had to be patient, as he found himself behind senior Jazz players such as Enes Kanter. He was also farmed out to NBA Development League team the Bakersfield Jam for periods during the season. He did play a part in all 82 games the next season, where he averaged 9.5 rebounds per game.

Gobert defends Orlando Magic center Nikola Vucevic in March 2018, helping land a 94–80 victory.

>>>>> FAST FACT >>>>>

Thanks to his 7'1" stature, 7'9" wingspan, 9'7" standing reach, and ability to stop almost any offense, Gobert has earned himself the nickname "The Stifle Tower."

WAITING HIS TURN

Coupled with his tactics and timing, Rudy's incredible anatomy makes him a formidable opponent under the basket on both defensive and offensive rebounding. Gobert stepped up his defensive game in the 2016–17 season, leading the league with an average 2.6 blocks per game. Hampered by injuries the following season, he still recorded a season-high 26 points against the Timberwolves in March 2018 and was in the NBA All-Defensive First Team, becoming only the third Jazz player to win multiple All-Defensive First Team recognition, and then went on to win the NBA Defensive Player of the Year award.

GREATEST OF ALL TIME

These guys may have **HUNG UP THEIR SNEAKERS** a long time ago, but they can still teach **TODAY'S SUPERSTARS** a thing or two about **RULING THE COURT.**

KAREEM ABDUL-JABBAR

D.O.B: APRIL 16, 1947 | **POSITION:** CENTER | **TEAMS:** MILWAUKEE BUCKS, L.A. LAKERS

With an NBA career that spanned an astonishing 20 seasons, Kareem used his trademark "skyhook" shot to ram home point after point and become the league's leading all-time scorer. By the time he left the game in 1989, he held records for most points scored (38,387), most games played (1,560), most career wins (1,074), and a long list of other records.

VS

SHAQUILLE O'NEAL

D.O.B: MARCH 6, 1972 | **POSITION:** CENTER | **TEAMS:** MAGIC, LAKERS, HEAT, SUNS, CAVALIERS, CELTICS

Are you ready for the "Shaq Attack?" At 7'1" tall and weighing in at 325 pounds, O'Neal was one of the biggest players on the court and knew how to make his presence felt. During his career, he led the NBA ten times in field goal percentage, and finished with a conversion accuracy for field goals on .582—one of the highest of all time!

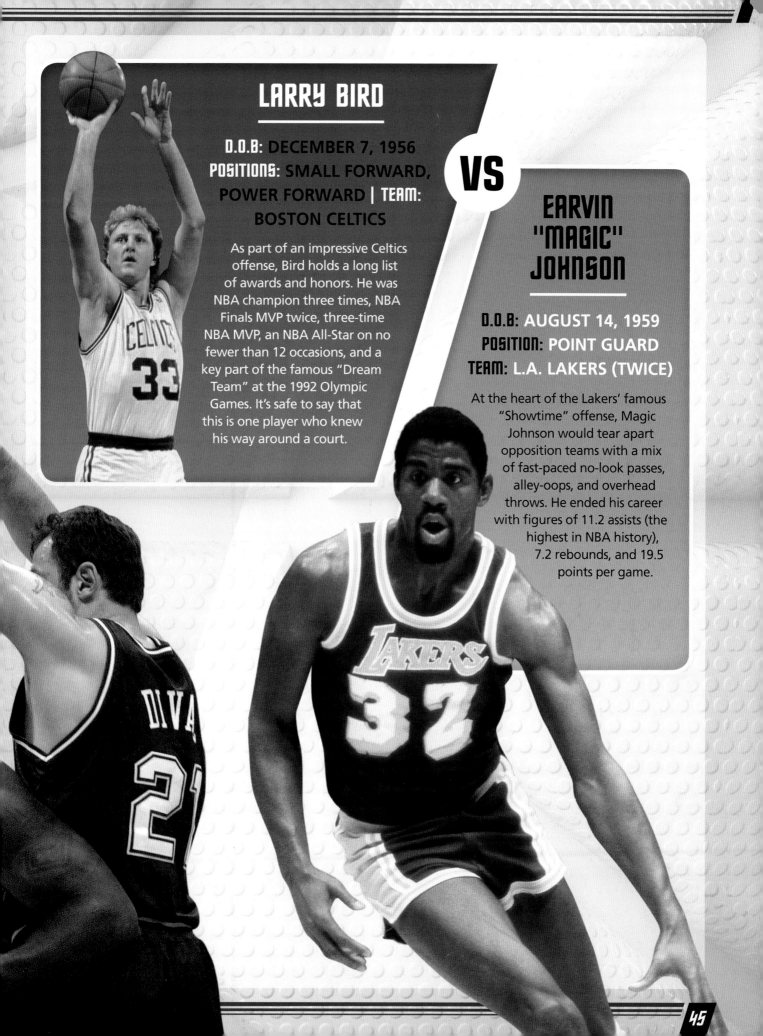

LARRY BIRD

D.O.B: DECEMBER 7, 1956
POSITIONS: SMALL FORWARD, POWER FORWARD | **TEAM:** BOSTON CELTICS

VS

As part of an impressive Celtics offense, Bird holds a long list of awards and honors. He was NBA champion three times, NBA Finals MVP twice, three-time NBA MVP, an NBA All-Star on no fewer than 12 occasions, and a key part of the famous "Dream Team" at the 1992 Olympic Games. It's safe to say that this is one player who knew his way around a court.

EARVIN "MAGIC" JOHNSON

D.O.B: AUGUST 14, 1959
POSITION: POINT GUARD
TEAM: L.A. LAKERS (TWICE)

At the heart of the Lakers' famous "Showtime" offense, Magic Johnson would tear apart opposition teams with a mix of fast-paced no-look passes, alley-oops, and overhead throws. He ended his career with figures of 11.2 assists (the highest in NBA history), 7.2 rebounds, and 19.5 points per game.

HOW WELL DO YOU KNOW THE NBA?

Test your knowledge of the NBA's star players and teams and see just how much you know. The answers are on page 48, but no cheating until you've finished the quiz!

1. HOW MANY OLYMPIC GOLD MEDALS HAS CHRIS PAUL WON?
- a) 1
- b) 3
- c) 2

2. WHICH TEAM WON THE 2017-18 NBA CHAMPIONSHIP?
- a) Golden State Warriors
- b) Cleveland Cavaliers
- c) Denver Nuggets

3. WHICH TWO NBA TEAMS DID NBA ALL-TIME GREAT MICHAEL JORDAN PLAY FOR?
- a) Cleveland Cavaliers and L.A. Lakers
- b) Washington Wizards and Chicago Bulls
- c) Denver Nuggets and Miami Heat

4. WHICH PORTLAND TRAIL BLAZERS PLAYER HAS THE NICKNAME "BIG GAME DAME?"
- a) Damian Lillard
- b) C.J. McCollum
- c) Meyers Leonard

5. STEPHEN CURRY AND KLAY THOMPSON FORM WHICH HIGH-SCORING PAIR?
- a) the "Crash Brothers"
- b) the "Trash Brothers"
- c) the "Splash Brothers"

6. FOR WHICH NBA TEAM DOES RUSSELL WESTBROOK PLAY AS POINT GUARD?
- a) Toronto Raptors
- b) Oklahoma City Thunder
- c) Boston Celtics

7. WHICH TEAM PICKED CHRIS PAUL DURING THE 2005 NBA DRAFT?
- a) Denver Nuggets
- b) New Orleans Hornets
- c) Sacramento Kings

8. HOW MANY TIMES HAS STEPHEN CURRY LED THE NBA IN FREE THROW PERCENTAGES?
- a) two times
- b) four times
- c) ten times

9. DURING THE 2016-17 SEASON, HOW MANY TIMES DID RUSSELL WESTBROOK RECORD 50 POINTS OR MORE?
- a) three times
- b) four times
- c) five times

10. WHICH TEAM DOES FINN LAURI MARKKANEN PLAY FOR?
- a) Chicago Bulls
- b) L.A. Lakers
- c) Boston Celtics

11. WHAT NUMBER DOES UTAH JAZZ SHOOTING GUARD DONOVAN MITCHELL WEAR ON HIS JERSEY?
- a) 23
- b) 17
- c) 45

12. HOW MANY YEARS DID LEBRON JAMES PLAY COLLEGE BASKETBALL FOR?
- a) 0 years
- b) 2 years
- c) 3 years

13. HOW MANY TIMES HAS LEBRON JAMES BEEN MADE NBA MVP DURING HIS CAREER SO FAR?
   a) once
   b) three times
   c) four times

14. KEVIN DURANT'S SCORING RECORD STANDS AT HOW MANY POINTS PER GAME?
   a) 27.1
   b) 32.4
   c) 50.8

15. WHAT WAS THE NAME OF KOBE BRYANT'S MOVIE FOR WHICH HE WON AN OSCAR?
   a) *Hoop Dreams*
   b) *Dear Football*
   c) *Dear Basketball*

16. WHICH COLLEGE TEAM DID ANTHONY DAVIS PLAY FOR?
   a) Kentucky Wildcats
   b) Texas Longhorns
   c) UCLA Bruins

17. WHAT DID THE SEATTLE SUPERSONICS CHANGE THEIR NAME TO IN 2008?
   a) Washington Wizards
   b) Oklahoma City Thunder
   c) Denver Nuggets

18. WHICH CAPITAL CITY WAS GIANNIS ANTETOKOUNMPO BORN IN?
   a) London, UK
   b) Moscow, Russia
   c) Athens, Greece

19. WHO, IN NOVEMBER 2017, BECAME THE YOUNGEST PLAYER IN NBA HISTORY TO REACH 700 MADE THREE-POINTERS?
   a) C.J. McCollum
   b) Bradley Beal
   c) LeBron James

20. C.J. MCCOLLUM IS SHOOTING GUARD FOR WHICH NBA TEAM?
   a) Portland Trail Blazers
   b) Houston Rockets
   c) Minnesota Timberwolves

21. KARL-ANTHONY TOWNS'S MOTHER HAILS FROM WHICH CARIBBEAN COUNTRY?
   a) Jamaica
   b) Cuba
   c) Dominican Republic

22. KNOWN AS "THE STIFLE TOWER," UTAH JAZZ CENTER RUDY GOLBERT IS FROM WHICH EUROPEAN COUNTRY?
   a) Germany
   b) France
   c) Spain

23. WHICH NBA TEAM DID NBA LEGEND LARRY BIRD PLAY FOR?
   a) L.A. Lakers
   b) Miami Heat
   c) Boston Celtics

24. WHAT WAS THE SIZE OF THE NEW CONTRACT OFFERED TO STEPHEN CURRY IN JULY 2017?
   a) $125 million
   b) $176 million
   c) $201 million

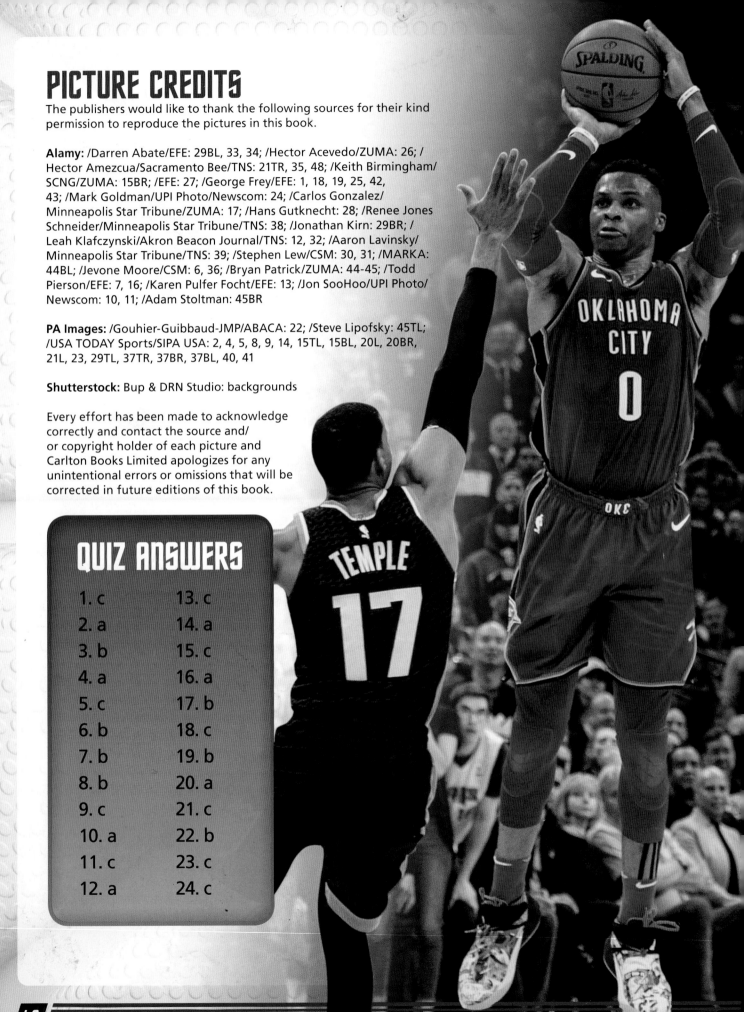

PICTURE CREDITS

The publishers would like to thank the following sources for their kind permission to reproduce the pictures in this book.

QUIZ ANSWERS

1. c	13. c
2. a	14. a
3. b	15. c
4. a	16. a
5. c	17. b
6. b	18. c
7. b	19. b
8. b	20. a
9. c	21. c
10. a	22. b
11. c	23. c
12. a	24. c